Hildegard Niemann

Budgerigars

Everything About Purchase, Care,
..., Behavior, and Training

Filled with full-color Photographs
by Oliver Giel

BARRON'S

Contents

The Typical Budgerigar

Budgerigars are fascinating creatures. The enthusiasm for these nimble and charming mini-exotics continues unabated, so that they are now among the most popular pets worldwide. Yet, what is it that makes these little Australian birds so irresistible?

Curious, Playful, and Sociable

When budgerigars were discovered in Australia, during an expedition by Captain James Cook in 1770, nobody could anticipate that these attractive little parrots would embark on a massive invasion into millions of homes worldwide. However, it took a while for the first budgerigars to arrive in Europe. It was not until 1840 that they finally commenced their victorious advance, when the famous naturalist John Gould brought the very first live budgerigars into England. Budgies reached the European continent about ten years later. There they became real survival artists: it took only a few years for the birds to start raising their young in Europe, which was a real sensation at that time. The wife of a German manufacturer managed the first successful German breeding—more accidentally than deliberately—using a coconut shell as a nest box. Since then, budgerigars have become one of the most popular pets in the world. It is estimated that more than 30 million budgerigars are kept as pets. Although these birds weigh only 1 to 2 ounces, they can reach a maximum life of 15 years when being taken care of properly. While the plumage of wild birds is characterized principally by the colors green, yellow, and black, there are nowadays many different color varieties: today prospective pet owners can select from among single-colored birds, pied-colored ones, or from a wide variety of different color combinations.

Entertaining Companions

While the social life of these little Australian birds is extremely complex, you can observe new and different aspects of this when you keep budgerigars as pets. These birds are very intelligent and interact actively with their environment. Sometimes, they will even learn to "talk," especially the males. These little energy bundles are curious and need to be kept very busy in order to stay fit. Moreover, each bird is different from the next, simply because every budgerigar has its very own character traits.

Budgerigars are not only ideal indoor birds for enthusiasts of Australian small parrots; because they are relatively easy to keep, they are also suitable for beginning parrot hobbyists, as well as for children, senior citizens, and those who are working full-time and do not have the time throughout the day to look after their pets. The effect budgerigars have on us humans is amazing.

American studies have shown that keeping budgerigars not only lowers blood pressure, but it also prevents depression. The reason: the owners of budgerigars are more likely to communicate among each other, because the common theme of "budgerigars" also opens up avenues for other topics of discussion. Anyone who decides to get a budgerigar is, in terms of his or her own character, very open and approachable to the people around him or her.

Perfect Roommates

Because budgerigars have a well-defined sociable vein, their owners will take them to heart very quickly. As such, they quickly become excellent "tenants" and with that an integral part of the family. There are many arguments in favor of these birds:

› as soon as you have gained the trust of your budgerigar there are absolutely no obstacles to having all sorts of fun and games for the two of you. Within a very short period of time the birds become hand-tame and very much enjoy being gently scratched, principally around the head; but they usually do not like to be touched anywhere else on the body.

› the noise level of budgerigars (compared to that of other parrots) is low, so that they are very suitable for keeping in a (rented) apartment. This makes things easy on the nerves of your neighbors!

Water is the elixir of life for wild budgerigars: it determines when the birds will breed and to where these little nomads will migrate.

> budgies are real family members: they are very curious and actively take part in family life.
> if budgies are kept in a small flock you will observe their courtship, jealousy dramas, intrigues, friendships, and close affections. The body language of budgerigars is surprisingly diverse and a lot of fun to observe.
> some budgerigars—especially males—will actually mimic words and sounds.
> the only disadvantage of budgerigars: there is going to be some dust and dirt. If you allow your birds free-flight time, the birds will leave small bird droppings, and, of course, leftover food, in their travels throughout the room. Even caged birds can make quite a mess, and you will need to vacuum on a regular basis (see page 51).

Australia: Home of Budgerigars

The original habitat of budgerigars is Australia. Nearly 70 percent of this continent consists of arid and semi-arid landscapes where it rarely ever rains. Therefore, the growth phases of plants in these areas are very short, often lasting merely a month or so. Only about two dozen bird species can survive under such difficult conditions, including the small budgerigar.

Budgerigars are extremely well adapted to such harsh conditions, because they belong to those few terrestrial birds that possess a large salt gland. This enables them to drink water from salt lakes; excess salt is subsequently discharged via this gland. The birds adjust to the constantly changing food supply by migrating as flying nomads throughout the land. Spinifex grasses and ground covering plants are their principal food sources. In the wild, budgerigars spend the entire day in search of such food, mainly early in the morning and again late in the afternoon.

Budgerigars—are they suitable for me?

Before you decide on a budgerigar as a pet, you must ask yourself the following questions:

LONG-TERM RESPONSIBILITY Budgerigars can age up to 15 years. Are you able to accept the responsibility to look after these birds for so long?

SOCIABILITY AND EXERCISE Budgerigars are social birds and require plenty of interaction. Do you have sufficient time to spend with your pet? If not, you might consider keeping a pair of budgies so they can provide each other company. Are you prepared to provide your birds a sufficiently roomy cage and a play-stand with plenty of ladders and toys to allow them to work off energy?

WORK AND DIRT Lost feathers, feces, and dust must be removed daily. Are you willing to perform these tasks? Are you suffering from an allergy?

COSTS The initial cage and equipment costs can run a few hundred dollars; ongoing food, toys, and veterinary expenses might amount to another couple of hundred dollars per year. Can you afford to spend this amount?

A Day in a Flock of Budgerigars

Anyone who has observed the behavior of budgerigars in the wild will appreciate the demands and requirements of the birds when kept as pets.

Never alone: Budgerigars love companionship and everything they do is done together with their siblings. After the early morning preening, the birds take off in a flock for their feeding grounds, loudly vocalizing. The size of the flock is variable. Sometimes there may only be small groups of ten birds, and then again flocks can consist of up to a hundred birds, and then there are also times when there may be very large aggregations of thousands of budgerigars. The synchronized flights of these giant flocks are overwhelming. In order to drink, budgerigars fly directly into ponds and other small waterholes, and emerge again from the water by

means of rapidly beating their wings. In a very large flock it often happens that some of the birds land on top of those who are already drinking. Regrettably, there are some drowning victims. Outside the breeding season these flocks do not establish a social structure, and the size of a flock is constantly changing. One group of budgerigars leaves a flock, to be replaced by new arrivals. Within a flock small subgroups often come together, for example, a group of fledged youngsters. During the breeding season groups of male budgerigars will often look for food together in order to feed their females and chicks.

Short distance fliers: Although budgerigars are very good flyers, they are unable to remain airborne over long distances, because their own body fat is insufficient as an energy source. To compensate for this, budgerigars make a series of successive but shorter flights to the next food source in order to conserve energy.

Resting in leafy trees: Budgerigars are commonly found in eucalyptus trees when they are resting. Their coloration and teardrop-shaped bodies make them virtually disappear among the tree foliage. These camouflages, together with rapid flight formations, afford flocks excellent protection against enemies.

Rapid Breeders

Birds in arid regions are frequently nomads that can breed at any time of the year. The unpredictability of rain in dry regions has led to the development of a reproductive mechanism that can be very quickly activated. Therefore, budgerigars can start

Having a siesta at midday is a must: during the hot period of the day budgerigars rest in trees. Their plumage, together with their teardrop-shaped body form, provide excellent camouflage.

Budgerigars seek out and need the contact of siblings, with whom they feed, play, and "roughhouse" together. The security in a flock protects them against enemies, gives them comfort, and increases their well-being. Therefore, it is always important to provide plenty of human or second bird companionship for your pet.

breeding as soon as the first raindrop falls and the food supply improves. These little birds like to breed close together, and so it can happen that there are several occupied nest hollows in a single branch. In order to be able to rear budgerigar chicks successfully in the wild, however, the budgerigars must be able to find an abundance of food for a period of at least three months. This is important because the young hatch successively and then become fully-fledged over a very long period of time. Since the environmental conditions are very harsh, not even half of the chicks survive. In order to compensate for such losses, male budgerigars become sexually mature at an age of 60 days. Therefore, the budgerigar is a real survivor with charm, as well as the ability to resist heat, drought, and hunger!

Budgerigar Portraits

They do not always have to be bright green or light blue—although budgerigars in these colors are always very attractive. Similarly appealing are the other color varieties, such as gray, cobalt, or the various pied varieties.

COBALT: In regards to color, budgies are referred to as blue series or green (sometimes yellow) series birds. Blue budgies come in three shades: sky blue, cobalt, and mauve (image shows a young male).

BRIGHT GREEN: This color variety is particularly close to the wild (original) coloration of budgerigars. When crossing bright green birds with other color varieties, the progeny are mostly green (image shows a young male).

OPALINE SKY BLUE WITH LIGHT-COLORED WINGS: For budgerigars of this color variety, the standard requires light to white wings and a body that is as intensively blue as possible. Usually there are "ghost markings" on the wings (image shows a female).

LIGHT-WINGED, BRIGHT GREEN OPALINE: Some color varieties, such as this one, are often linked to a particular sex. This one was formerly known as "brown wing" (image shows a female).

AUSTRALIAN VIOLET PIED: It was not until the 1950s that this color mutation occurred among Australian breeders. The coloration is based on an irregular loss of the color pigment melanin (image shows a male).

GRAY: Gray coloration is due to strongly pigmented feathers that absorb most of the light, and so cannot reflect shades of blue (image shows a male).

YELLOW-FACED, DARK BLUE OPALINE: These budgerigars often have bright colors and are usually somewhat smaller than their siblings. The wave-like markings in their nape are often interrupted (image shows a male).

AUSTRALIAN PIED YELLOW, LIGHT BLUE FACE: The flight feathers, wings, and tail are rather light colored in this particular variety. Australian pieds also occur in many other colors and color combinations (image shows a male).

Alone or As a Duo? Male or Female?

In the wild, the flock provides individual budgerigars with security; in your home this responsibility lies with you. Your budgie will consider its human housemates as its "flock," and will want to spend a great deal of time interacting with you. If you choose to keep a single pet budgie, please keep this in mind and be certain to provide enough time to satisfy your pet's emotional needs as well as its physical ones. If, however, your schedule is packed and time is at a premium, consider purchasing at least two budgerigars. Your pet will then have a playmate for those times when you are too busy to

be around. Whether you decide on a pair or two males or females is entirely up to you. A pair will likely attempt to breed, so if you're not interested in increasing your flock size then stick to same sex pairs. When putting a mixed flock together it is important to make sure that the sex ratio is even. If there is an excess of females, it can lead to bloody arguments when the females want to breed. On the other hand, if males are in the majority there are essentially no problems. In any case, purchasing a budgerigar as a pet is essentially a question of individual taste and empathy toward a particular bird. Male budgerigars are slightly more talkative than females, but have a tendency to become less active when old. Female budgerigars have a strongly developed "chewing instinct" and should have access to a lot of soft wood.

Budgerigars and Children

Budgerigars are ideal pets for children. Keeping birds will teach children responsibility and how to care for another living being. Of course, the bottom line is that the parents will always have the principal responsibility for the birds. At an age of eight to ten years, children are generally capable of taking care of their first budgerigar. As the next step you need to impress upon the children that budgerigars are generally afraid of anything that is larger than they are, and that moves or comes at

Even when budgerigars belong to the children, the responsibility and welfare for these small Australian birds always remain with the parents.

1 ONLY DOGS that obey the command "NO" may approach the bird under strict supervision. Barking and romping around scare a budgerigar.

2 FOR CATS, birds are always prey: a friendship is always out of the question. Bites and scratches from a cat are life-threatening to a budgerigar and must be attended to by a veterinarian.

3 RABBITS AND GUINEA PIGS generally get along well with budgerigars. Nevertheless, such a mixed group must always be closely monitored.

them from above. For that reason you need to be very considerate when handling budgies. The first few weeks in a new home will decide whether a stable relationship of trust will develop between child and bird (see page 26). There is a simple method to quickly teach children to respect the "territorial boundary" of budgerigars: a strip of colored masking tape on the floor delineates the zone from whereon the birds start to become nervous. It demarcates the "personal space" of budgerigars. Within this zone the children have to move slowly and talk soothingly to the birds. At the beginning it is important for you, together with the child, to take care of the budgerigars. Later on the child is permitted to look after the bird on his or her own. However, you must always monitor whether the requirements of the budgerigars have been met.

Budgerigars and Other Pets

As prey animals, wild budgerigars are under constant pressure to avoid predators. Therefore, other pets are not necessarily suitable as companion animals for budgerigars.

Dogs and cats are among the natural enemies of birds. Budgerigars must never be left alone in a room with dogs or cats, not even when the door of the budgerigars' cage is closed. Dogs can push up against the cage, bark at it, or topple it over. Cats tend to jump on top of the cage and attempt to reach for the bird through the wire bars.

Guinea pigs and dwarf rabbits get along well with budgerigars. But it is important for you to make sure that the birds do not come into contact with the food of the other animals, since bacteria present in their mucus can be harmful for the birds.

Rats and mice should not be permitted in direct contact with budgerigars; these rodents can inflict serious bites and can carry pathogenic bacteria.

Snakes and ferrets are dangerous predators, and should never be allowed around pet birds.

Golden Rules for Buying a Budgerigar

You have decided on buying a budgerigar; now the search starts for a suitable bird. Take your time and make sure that the bird comes from a reliable and competent source.

Specialist pet shops: A good pet shop should have an overall clean appearance; the cages, and food and water containers of the budgerigars are clean; and the birds have various toys available to them. Budgerigars that have been kept in small box cages usually have an underdeveloped flight musculature and are prone to diseases. Therefore, it is advisable to purchase budgerigars from pet shops where the birds are kept in flight aviaries.

Budgerigar breeders: Budgerigars are often bred by hobbyists. If you purchase your bird from a reliable breeder, there is the advantage that the breeder can tell you a lot about the peculiarities and characteristics of your future pet. Another positive aspect: often these breeders will look after your birds while you are out of town.

Animal shelters: Another good supply source of a new budgerigar is the local animal shelter. The selection of birds available from such a facility is usually not large, but these surrendered birds usually have a sad life history; they deserve the care and attention from a devoted owner.

Advertisements: Often newspapers and bulletin boards carry advertisements offering budgerigars. Here it is important to closely examine the bird to ascertain whether there are any problems, and you should insist on being given the entire history of the budgie you are considering taking in.

After the purchase, all newly acquired budgerigars should be immediately examined by a veterinarian specializing in exotic birds or other small pets in order to ascertain the overall health condition of the bird. This gives you the opportunity to become acquainted with an experienced veterinarian who may also be helpful to you in the future.

Still living with Mom: only when Budgerigar babies are old enough to feed themselves may they move into a new home.

"Teeny" Budgie or Senior Bird?

Budgerigars are available in all age categories, and for each of these groups certain aspects need to be taken into consideration.

Young budgerigars can be purchased from an age of six to seven weeks onward. Their large black-button eyes, the wavelike markings that extend up to the wax-like, featherless *cere* (the area above the beak that contains the nostrils), and their dark beak make these feathered goblins simply irresistible. At that age, juvenile budgies adapt easily to new surroundings and it is not difficult for them to develop trust toward their new owner. Make sure that these young birds are fully fledged and that they are able to feed on their own. If they are not yet fully fledged they will stay hungry for the first few days. Hunger is certainly not a good basis for a friendly relationship between a budgerigar and its owner. Children should generally be given young birds. Older birds would place too much of a demand on children, because the change to a new owner makes them initially uneasy.

Older budgerigars generally require more time than younger birds to establish a relationship of trust with their new owner. It is possible that such budgerigars have had unpleasant experiences in the past or they have lived for an extended period in an aviary without direct contact with people; now they require more time in order to adjust to new surroundings. However, with patience, humor, and tender loving care these budgies will eventually become happy family members.

Neglected and sick budgerigars should only be purchased by experienced hobbyists. These birds have special requirements and will need permanent veterinary care, and they may never be able to associate normally with humans.

Fit from Beak to Tail

TIPS FROM THE
BUDGERIGAR EXPERT
Hildegard Niemann

EYES Shiny, clean, black in juveniles and with a yellow ring in older birds.

PLUMAGE Clean, shiny, and dense, tail and primary wing feathers must not be absent.

BEAK Smooth and well formed.

CERE Clean, without signs of discharge, pus, or scabs.

FEET Clean and smooth with healthy, scaly skin, two toes pointing forward and two pointing backward, short claws that can securely grab a branch.

CLOACA Clean feathers around the cloaca, without any fecal remnants or reddening.

FECAL BALLS (droppings) With clearly delineated white uric acid component, greenish feces, and watery urine. (Note: Fecal droppings can temporarily change color due to certain food items consumed, but a color change that lasts more than a few hours can indicate disease.)

BEHAVIOR The birds should be able to fly reliably, and run quickly and purposely on the ground, and they should display interest in their surroundings. A bird that is "fluffed up" and sits lethargically on a perch with its legs well apart, is sick and must immediately be taken to a veterinarian.

Anatomy and Sensory Perception

Plumage

Budgerigars are high-performance fliers. Their plumage and their rather long tail enable them to maneuver quickly. The plumage protects them against cold and the effects of intense solar radiation. In spite of that, the plumage makes up only 5 to 10 percent of their body weight.

Wings

The wings in free-living budgerigars are nearly 4 inches (10 cm) long. They are by far the most important locomotor mechanism these birds have. Properly functioning wings are something like "life insurance" for these birds: they are able to escape from predators only when they are able to fly properly and at maximum speed. The wings also play an important role in the body language of budgerigars.

Tail

In budgies the tail is their "rudder." It consists of 12 tail feathers (*retrices*), two internal (steering) tail feathers, and 10 outer (steering) tail feathers. All in all, it makes up nearly one half of their body length.

Claws

Budgerigars have two toes pointing forward and two pointing toward the back, all equipped with claws. Coloration of legs and feet can be variable. Birds that have been kept in an aviary usually have slightly darker legs than budgerigars that are kept always indoors.

Eyes

The eyes of young budgerigars are black. During puberty the eyes develop a whitish-yellow ring around their circumference. The eyes are located alongside the head, so these birds have almost all-around vision.

Beak

The beak is an important tactile organ and tool. Budgies use it to open seeds and keep in physical contact with their surroundings. The beak is also indispensable as a climbing aid and for grooming. Since it grows constantly throughout their life, budgerigars need a lot of branches to chew on, in order to wear their beaks down.

The Perfect Home for Birds

When they are given what they need, budgerigars are rather uncomplicated companions. A secure cage, room for free-flying or a play-stand for climbing, fascinating toys, comfortable perches, and a healthy diet—these are the prerequisites for the bird's contentment.

What Do Budgerigars Need?

Budgerigars are birds with character, and not simply little parrots, like many of the others. And yet all have the same basic requirements. As birds from an arid region they are not particularly demanding, and enjoy even minor attentiveness. Nevertheless, nothing but the best should be good enough for your pets.

> Select a cage suitable for budgerigars. For instance, sometimes budgies refuse to go into their cage because there are no toys and the birds are bored and lonely in their cage (see page 20).

> Even with only a modest degree of handiness you can construct little toys and extra perch sites yourself. What is important is that safety is always of primary concern. Cheap toys and secondhand cages are definitely taboo for your budgies.

> Be certain to provide a variety of perch styles and textures for the bird. Make sure that there are perches of variable thickness available in the cage and at the various extra landing sites around the room if you allow free flight.

> A healthy diet assures that your budgies are brimming with energy and will actually do somersaults when they are free-flying in the room, while loudly vocalizing. On the other hand, budgerigars that have been given an insufficient diet can only fly over short distances and will spend most of the day resting lethargically on a branch.

> Healthy and energetic budgerigars are very curious and need to investigate everything; they crawl into every hole and enjoy playing with their owner. Quality time out of the cage, either in free flight for fully flighted birds, or climbing on a play-stand for wing-clipped birds, will keep your pet exercised, tired, and contented.

Basic Equipment for Your Budgie

Budgerigars need a large cage or an indoor aviary. We cannot permit our birds to fly freely and unsupervised when we are not at home; the dangers of these little energy bundles sustaining an injury are simply too great. A large cage sufficiently equipped with toys and ample climbing opportunities is the ideal playroom for your budgerigars, where they will be safe and protected. Such a cage is a real adventure playground for your budgies, where there are new things to be discovered every day. At the same time it is also a wonderful and peaceful oasis to return to after any out-of-cage time. Climbing poles and ladders are valuable aids, especially for older budgerigars or those with joint problems. It helps them to get from one place to the next without having to fly. Sitting ropes are also popular among budgerigars. They can be bent in all directions and therefore provide an excellent, different climbing facility.

1 Cage

The cage should be made up of high-quality plated or powder-coated metal. These bars should be arranged horizontally along two sides and vertically on the other two sides, with two or three cross members so that the birds must use their wings a little when they are working their way up the bars. A large cage door with an integrated perch makes the cage an inviting playground during the free-flying period. A pair of birds should be given a cage with the approximate dimensions of $2\frac{3}{4} \times 1\frac{1}{2} \times 5\frac{1}{4}$ feet ($85 \times 50 \times 160$ cm); a group of four to six budgerigars need a cage of about $6 \times 1\frac{1}{2} \times 5\frac{1}{4}$ feet ($170 \times 50 \times 160$ cm). It is important that the cage is longer rather than high.

2 Foraging

Looking for food on the ground is a natural activity for budgerigars. In order to satisfy this instinct, you can provide your budgies with a small bowl of clean sand or gravel with some seed mixed in. Place this dish in a spot that is unlikely to collect droppings from above. So that the budgerigars do not end up looking for food among their own droppings, the dish must be emptied and cleaned daily.

3 Toys

Budgerigars require a lot of physical activity. Consequently, toys, swings, climbing spirals, and triangles must always be present in a cage. Make sure that these items are installed correctly: spiral and swing must always be attached at the highest point of the cage, and locate the toys next to the perch in such a way that birds can easily play with them.

4 Feed containers

Food containers made of stainless steel are ideal. Plastic containers eventually become scratched, offering bacteria easy settlement sites. Buy yourself two or even three sets of cups so when you are pressed for time you can feed quickly and cleanly without any problems.

5 Beak grinding stone or cuttlebone

A limestone rock or cuttlefish bone is used for supplying calcium and as a beak grinding stone. One should always be present in the cage when keeping budgerigars. Mature females especially require additional calcium supplements. Attach this stone next to a perch, so that it can easily be reached by the budgies.

Budgerigars Are Happy Here!

Not only the equipment of a budgerigar cage is important, but also the location is important for the birds to feel safe and secure.

› The best location is in a corner of the room, opposite the entrance door; however, NEVER on a windowsill or directly next to a door. The optimum location would be in a living or dining room, where there is maximum contact with the entire family.

› Caged budgerigars dislike direct exposure to sunlight, and can become dangerously overheated. When the birds are being kept in a very bright room, make sure that they can readily withdraw into the shade.

Play Stands for Active Pets

Your budgie will enjoy active time out with the family. If you do not wish to allow free flight, have your veterinarian or bird groomer periodically clip the bird's flight feathers. Wing clips are painless (much like getting a haircut) and will temporarily restrict the bird's ability to fly. It will regain flight capability as soon as new flight feathers grow in, so wing clips need to be repeated once or twice a year as the bird molts. To ensure that your clipped bird gets plenty of quality exercise, provide a play stand with ladders, climbing rings, and other active toys. Encourage your pet to play, and it will get a good workout romping on the stand.

Landing Sites for Free Flight

Every free-flying budgerigar needs at least one safe landing site outside of the cage, either suspended or freestanding. It serves merely as a place to land for the bird, but it should also offer ample opportunities for various activities. You can offer fruit and vegetables to your pets while they are there, and so it becomes a bit of a climbing facility at the same time. Spirals and coconut shells or little baskets made of untreated willow branches are easy to attach below the cage ceiling, and serve as a playground and hide food. Suspended landing sites must never be placed close to doors, because of the risk of injury to the bird.

The easy way to sit: natural branches that massage sensitive foot soles and grind down the claws as the bird runs along the perch.

Rope artist: Perching ropes encourage climbing and swinging. Fibers and threads must be cut off daily, so that budgie claws do not become entangled in them.

Twice the pleasure: rocking, swinging, and hanging are enjoyed by all budgerigars, and if a treat, like parsley, is also involved—better yet!

Perfect Perching Opportunities

Ideal perches are made from natural branches. Perches made from round dowels or out of plastic can harm the feet of your budgerigars and lead to painful sores, because the birds always sit on the perches with the same foot position. The solution is using one or two natural branches, a climbing rope, and a sand or cement "pedicure perch" attached in the lower third of the cage, where the birds can wear down their claws.

Diversity Is Essential

It is now recommended to place up to five toys in budgerigar cages. Obviously, two budgerigars with five toys and various landing facilities will require a sufficiently large cage. In order to avoid boredom setting in, you should exchange the toys once a week. Only the favorite toys should be left in the cage. Please remember to check the toys daily for possible safety problems. For young birds who are still timid, you should wait with changing toys until

a degree of trust has been established. Only after the young birds are no longer afraid of your hand, can you work inside the cage with the young birds still in it.

Helpful Tip: Frightened as well as calm birds should be given toys that are large enough so that they can hide behind them. Budgerigars like to withdraw if the family activities around them are overwhelming.

Avoiding Stress from the Start

When a bird is stressed out or is constantly being chased away from a perch or from a food container by another bird, this could be due to inadequate cage arrangement. Maybe the perches are too far down, the swings are too high up, or the birds are becoming entangled in toys. If you cannot find a specific cause for such behavior in order to eliminate it, it is best to seek the advice of a behavioral therapist.

Welcome to the New Home

The big day has arrived; you are bringing your pet budgerigar home. Arrange for gentle transport, so that the start into a life together is successful. Budgerigars are often "packed" in closed cardboard boxes that have ventilating slots; however, it is far safer for the bird to travel in a small transport box made of plastic. These boxes have a door that opens out, and they can be re-used later for the trip to the veterinarian for the annual check-up. Make sure that the box is not in direct sun when transporting the bird in a car. Place the carrier on a seat and fasten securely behind a safety belt.

At home you should have prepared the cage in advance with food and drinking water, so that the bird can move straight in. Open the transport box and place it at the bottom of the cage. Your budgie will soon emerge and then initially flutter, intimidated, around in the cage. Step a few paces back from the cage so that the bird can settle down as quickly as possible.

During the first few hours your budgie will be frightened and nervous. This is quite a normal reaction to the transport. After a while the bird will start to smoothen out its plumage and it may even eat a few seeds. A first climb through the cage will help with its orientation in the new home. Now the bird starts to explore its new environment. Even though it may be difficult for you and your family to restrain yourselves, give the budgerigar some peace during its first day with you! In particular, observe whether the budgerigar drinks sufficiently and displays an interest in its new surroundings. A bird that sits lethargically on the bottom of the cage must be taken immediately to the veterinarian! Transport stress could have exacerbated a latent infection.

Visits from friends to your house should be put on hold for a few days until the budgie has settled in. Wait with the acquisition of a second bird until the first one has become accustomed to the new surroundings and is integrated into the family. This goes quicker when the bird is not preoccupied with a companion. As soon as the bird has developed trust in you, the second bird should be purchased. Keep the second bird isolated from the first one for at least two (but preferably four) weeks. Such a quarantine period helps to protect the first bird from any diseases, and gives you the opportunity to establish a relationship with the second bird. When you are certain that the second bird is fit, you can put both birds together.

When the *Cage* Becomes a *Refuge*

Never force a budgerigar out of its cage. A budgie that does not want to leave its cage suffers from "cage-bonding syndrome." The bird has had traumatic experiences and has lost its sense of security. Be very patient with such a bird and offer help. Place food on a branch next to the cage door, and turn your head to one side—this indicates to the bird that you do not intend to harm it.

The First Few Weeks at Home

Budgerigars prefer routines; they give them a feeling of security. Therefore, feed the birds every day at the same time and be very gentle with them. **Remove any fears.** When you do any maintenance work on or inside the cage, turn your head slightly to one side. We humans have a face like that of a predator; our eyes are pointing directly forward, our nose is very large, and from the perspective of a budgerigar we have giant hands. When we turn our head sideways, this visual scheme disappears and our birds can relax. Hum a bit or talk to the budgies in a soft voice, so that they become accustomed to your voice.

Initially, children should play with the budgies only under parental supervision, because sudden movements and roughhousing of any sort scare budgerigars and so make the adjustment for the birds to their new home and family more difficult. **Rest is important.** Make sure that the budgerigars are getting enough sleep. If the birds get frightened in the dark, injuries can occur, because the birds flutter wildly around inside the cage and cannot see the perches. A night-light is usually the answer for situations like these.

Getting Used to Other Pets

If you also own other pets, you should have your budgie get used to them; this takes a lot of patience!

Other birds: In a flock, budgerigars readily integrate with other small parrot species. There should not be any problems, but be aware of bullying by other birds.

Always on top: budgerigars like to perch on the highest points. They feel safe there and can see everything.

Dogs, cats, and other predatory pets:
Budgerigars are scared of dogs and cats. Speak calmly to your bird when a dog or a cat is also in the room, and be explicit to the latter that budgerigars are not prey. Even so, the predatory instinct is hard to control, even in the tamest pets. Therefore do not, under any circumstances, allow your budgie out of its cage when dogs, cats, snakes, or ferrets are present.

The First Time Out

The very first time out of the cage is an adventure for the budgerigar as well as for its owner (see page 38).

Firstly, make sure that all windows and doors are closed and inform all family accordingly. Safely

confine other pets. If you want your budgie to remain on a play stand, be certain that its wings are properly clipped. If you are allowing free flight, remove any objects that could pose a danger, and remove or cover any open water containers. Initially, the budgerigars will be somewhat timid and hesitant to land on very high objects. Yet, with a few tricks and some patience the birds will gradually become hand-tame:

⟩ Relax and read something, so that your budgies can familiarize themselves with their new surroundings in peace.

⟩ As soon as the birds are feeding and relaxed next to you, keep talking to them gently while slowly placing your hand next to the millet.

⟩ Then, start to raise your hand slowly. Eventually it becomes normal for the budgerigars to see your hand moving, and they will finally lose their shyness.

1 ESTABLISH TRUST Approach the cage slowly, indirectly, and in a wide arc, all the while talking to your budgie. If it pulls back, stand still and wait until the bird relaxes again. When the bird accepts your closeness, try attracting it with millet. Praise it while it is feeding. Repeat this exercise several times daily, until the bird has become used to it.

2 APPROACHING As soon as your budgerigar appears to be pleased to see you approaching, open the cage door slightly so that the bird does not get scared. Once the cage door is opened sufficiently wide, give the millet with one hand and offer the other hand as a perch for the bird to sit on. When the bird comes to the hand that holds the millet, give your budgie praise in abundance. Practice this several times every day, but never put any pressure on the bird.

3 FIRST STEPS Once the budgerigar accepts the hand as a perch, slowly remove the bird from the cage. Commands, such as "UP" and "DOWN," indicate to the bird how it is to react and makes communication easier. Treats are mainly given when the bird comes to you. Talk a lot and show the bird how pleased you are that he trusts you.

The Proper Diet for Fit Birds

Budgerigars have a tendency toward becoming overweight and then incur health problems associated with excess weight. The energy requirement of your budgerigar depends on its size, the amount of activity it has enjoyed, and whether the bird lives together with a companion or in a flock—life in a flock requires more energy. You should have their physical condition assessed by a veterinarian once a year.

The Perfect Grain Mix

The basic food of all budgerigars is a balanced grain mixture, for example, 45 percent various millets (large, or hairy, crabgrass [*Digitaria sanguinalis*], foxtail millet [*Selaria italica*]), 25 percent Proso Millet [*Panicum miliaceum*], and 25 percent canary seeds. The remaining 5 percent can consist of oats, which can also be given when germinated. Often seed mixtures are available in shops in open bins for do-it-yourself mixing. Such containers are ideal breeding grounds for the larvae of mill or flour moths and other food pests. Therefore, you should select food sealed in plastic packages and always check the use-by date. Once the bag has been opened, the food should be stored in a cool, dark, and dry place, such as in a refrigerator, freezer, or pantry. Never use moldy-smelling or fungus-covered food to feed your birds. If you are in doubt about the quality of the food, throw it out and purchase a fresh bag. A new bag of seed is much less costly than a vet visit! Always give grain feed early in the morning and again late in the afternoon; this way you imitate the natural daily feeding sequence of budgerigars in the wild. If you want your budgie's day to be a bit more exciting, you can give the morning grain ration mixed in with the sand in a sand bowl. This way the bird has to search for its food and pick it out from among the sand grains. But in the evening the budgerigar should be able to eat as much as it likes to get it through the night.

Vitamins and More

Throughout the day you should give your budgies plenty of green feed, vegetables, and fruit to keep them busy. You should avoid crackers and other calorie-rich treats, because these will make your birds fat. Only under exceptional circumstances, for example, after an illness, should the birds be given such a treat.

Spray millet: This is the favorite treat for all budgerigars. You should use it principally for training purposes. Your budgies should know that you are the person who gives them these treats. This intensifies trust and supports bonding.

For Well-rounded Nutrition

COMMERCIAL BUDGIE SEED MIXTURES contain many small seeds that are similar to the natural food of budgies in the wild. These mixes are sometimes fortified with vitamins and minerals, and are a nutritious alternative to blending your own diets. Formulated (pelleted) diets are also designed for budgies, and can be a valuable addition to a healthy diet.

HEALTHY FOOD Herbs provide lots of vitamins and minerals. But there are also additional benefits: they keep the birds busy and active. For instance, dandelion is rich in vitamin A. Feed the leaves before the plants start to flower, because flowering dandelions taste bitter. Chickweed grows nearly everywhere, but you must collect it only from clean (non-contaminated) sites. Herbs grown in pots on the windowsill are an excellent source of vitamins during the winter months.

SWEET FRUITS Budgerigars are particular when it comes to fruit. They love apples and pears, but soft fruit is usually rejected. Fruits offer many vitamins and minerals, as well as needed fiber. Offer fruit only for a limited time, since it spoils fairly quickly, and give only fruit pieces, because the birds will have to gnaw on them and that keeps them busy. Of course, it goes without saying: all fruit needs to be washed before it is fed to the birds, and avoid those fruits that have been sprayed with chemicals.

VEGETABLES ARE ESSENTIAL You should offer at least three different types every day. Hard kohlrabi and carrots can remain in the cage all day, while soft cucumbers must be removed after a few hours.

Fruits and vegetables: Both are important supplements for the diet of your budgerigars. From among the fruits, budgies seem to prefer the hard types; apples and pears are their favorites. But they are also rather fond of vegetables. Carrots are important providers of vitamin A, as well as being wonderful toys—using toothpicks, you can attach carrots pieces to cucumbers and zucchini. Alternately, you can also wrap carrot strips (cut with a peeler) around individual bars of the cage. Similarly, broccoli and cauliflower can be turned into ideal toys. Instead of rolling a ball along the bottom of its cage, your budgie can roll small Brussels sprouts. Beets are also very popular, but the disadvantage is that they strongly discolor everything with which they come into contact. So, do not be surprised when you end up with a budgie that has a red face—the bird has enjoyed its meal. Afterwards, the droppings are often brownish, which does not need to worry you. Tomatoes and capsicums (paprika) can lead to crop problems in sensitive birds, and so these vegetables should be avoided.

Wild greens: These are a nice addition to the diet of budgerigars. They are low in calories, but vitamin-rich and they provide excellent opportunities for physical activities for the birds. Apart from chickweed, shepherd's purse, and perennial ryegrass (*Lolium perenne*), you can also use common knotgrass (especially its blossoms), plantains, millet rice (barnyard grass), finger millet, and yellow foxtail (millet). Another treat is common sorrel, but unfortunately it is only available in spring. Budgerigars are particularly fond of the flowers and the fresh seeds.

Herbs: A range of common herbs that have not been sprayed with chemicals, such as parsley, common sorrel, watercress, and basilica are available throughout the year from the vegetable section of your supermarket. These are an important alternative when wild herbs are not available during the winter. Place a little herb pot into a food container holder inside the cage, and soon your birds will enjoy the green diet.

Helpful Tip: Make sure you thoroughly clean and wash all fruits and vegetables before feeding them to your birds. They must never have been in contact with insecticides or herbicides; the immune system of your budgies cannot handle such highly toxic substances. If you are in doubt, you can get these fresh food items from an organic food store.

1 It tastes better with company! The budgerigars will enjoy their favorite seeds first. Later they will de-husk the remaining seeds.

2 Anyone who wants to nibble on a treat has to work for it. Budgerigars should have to do gymnastics or fly in order to enjoy a treat, like millet.

29

Avoid Feeding Mistakes

TIPS FROM THE
BUDGERIGAR EXPERT
Hildegard Niemann

AVOCADOS must never be fed, not even in small pieces, because they are toxic for budgerigars. Pass this information on to all budgerigar keepers to avoid deadly mistakes.

WILD PLANTS Never collect these from alongside roads, streets, or intersections. The concentration of harmful pollutants is too high.

SAFFLOWER AND SUNFLOWER SEEDS Avoid seed mixtures containing high amounts of safflower or sunflower seeds! These seeds contain large amounts of fats, which can lead to vascular and cardiac problems in budgerigars.

HEMP Hemp should not be present in commercial seed mixtures for non-breeding birds. Like many birds that breed when environmental conditions are favorable, budgerigars react to hemp with elevated hormone levels.

INCORRECT FEEDING Sometimes incorrect feeding can cause non-stop egg laying in females, a life-threatening condition. These females become exhausted and the condition finally leads to a calcium deficiency.

Water

Water is of elementary importance to the health of your budgerigars.

› Make sure that your birds always have clean drinking water available. Change the water at least twice a day. Bottled drinking water bought in stores is usually not necessary; however, if your home is using private well water, or if you have any reason to question its purity, bottled water is a good alternative.

› A drinking water dispenser with a long tube is unsuitable because it is difficult to clean, and small (dirty) gaps are ideal breeding grounds for bacteria. On the other hand, water containers made of stainless steel can easily be cleaned or simply put into a dishwashing machine.

› Many publications suggest that vitamin and mineral supplements should be added to the drinking water of budgerigars. That is nonsense. Due to their special metabolism, budgerigars are able to do without drinking water for a prolonged period, provided fresh food is available to them; yet, not having an available water supply is unhealthy for your birds. Vitamins and minerals dissolved in water will deteriorate quickly under the influence of light, and will thus lose their effectiveness. These added nutrients will enhance the reproduction of bacteria, which will then be deposited along the bottom of the water container. Always use vitamin/mineral supplements in powdered form, which can easily be sprinkled onto food. Remember to remove uneaten portions after an hour or two to prevent bacterial growth.

› Do not administer medications via drinking water unless directed to do so by your veterinarian; their effectiveness is doubtful when the amount that the budgerigar takes in cannot be controlled.

Establishing Trust Right from the Start

Initially your budgerigars will feel insecure and frightened; however, if you follow a few important behavior rules and are aware of your body language, the ice will soon be broken.

. . . and what not to do!

Always approach the cage with your face slightly turned away, constantly talking to the birds, so that they become used to your voice.

Prepare all family members for the arrival of the new pets, and set up important rules for their future behavior toward the birds.

Permit free flight only under supervision. The danger to the birds of sustaining an injury during an unsupervised free flight is too great.

Set up a list of contacts with emergency telephone numbers of your veterinarian, including after-hours numbers, vacation substitutes, and a behavioral therapist.

Never ignore your budgerigar or neglect its emotional needs. If you cannot provide plenty of daily interaction, consider adding a second bird for company.

During the first few days you should do without visitors and other hectic activities around the cage, so that your budgerigars do not feel insecure.

Never leave your dog, cat, ferret, or snake alone with the budgerigars. This could lead to serious accidents.

Never catch the budgerigars by hand, because this terrifies the birds. Hands are supposed to give confidence.

A Harmonious Relationship

Life with budgerigars makes for a lot of pleasure—these little feathered fellows are even-tempered and intelligent, curious and quick, sensible and sensitive. One thing is for sure: there is never any boredom in their company.

Action, Play, and Excitement

Budgerigars love company. All activities are done with a partner, be it man or sibling. Once the trust between the birds and the family has been established, the budgies will help your children with homework, be by your side when you are cleaning the vegetables for lunch, or simply join you for an evening of comfortable television viewing.

Always in Good Spirits

Budgerigars are known for their good mood and temperament, and their joy of life. It is rarely ever totally quiet when you share your life with these feathered sprites. Their curiosity, intelligence, and playfulness are unique. Budgerigars will greet you in the morning with their happy twitter and will accompany breakfast radio with enthusiastic singing. These parrots in miniature format follow all your activities with their searching eyes, and indeed will follow you anywhere. If you are doing something that is of particular interest to the birds, they will run down your arm in order to see better; and if you are doing something the birds dislike, they will use all their energy in small interference maneuvers.

Life in a Budgie Clan

Should there be a time that you cannot make yourself available for your budgerigars, they will play with their sibling or simply groom each other. In a small flock, pairs will form, there will be arguments and reconciliations, an amorous male will break the hearts of females, jealousy dramas will take place, and close friendships will be made; all that is integrated in the natural life cycle of budgerigars.

Good Friends with Your Budgerigar

The sensory organs of budgerigars are highly developed. For that reason, budgerigars are distinctly alert and sharp contemporaries when we share our life with them—nothing eludes a budgerigar. The eyes, located laterally on the head, provide for an almost complete 360-degree view. Also, the feet are equipped with tiny sensory cells that perceive the slightest vibration. Therefore, you need not attempt to approach a budgerigar

unnoticed—you will have no chance. And their sensible character, intelligence, and mimicking ability assure that something like a real friendship can develop between man and bird.

First and Foremost: Good Communication

Budgerigars love communicating, and it is rarely quiet when you share your life with budgerigars. Moreover, budgies are not simply just babbling, but instead they communicate with their partner, be it man or bird. Today we know that budgerigars talk very much faster than, for instance, man; so there is much our budgerigars have already mastered that we cannot understand. It is simply spoken too fast. Moreover, these little Australians have also developed their own dialect, spoken by the entire flock. This can easily be observed when a new bird is joining the flock; initially, the new bird will be very quiet and listen attentively to the sounds given off by the flock. Once it has learned this new dialect it will eagerly participate in the flock "discussion." Here it is interesting to note that females have their own contact call that has to be learned by respective males. Females never learn the contact calls of males; the "ladies" are rather demanding in this respect!

A talk among friends: male budgerigars are generally more talkative and more sociable than female budgerigars.

Are we speaking the same dialect? Budgerigars are attentive listeners and will quickly learn the sounds made around them.

Having Fun Teaching Your Bird to Talk

PRACTICE with your budgies only when you are in a good mood. Never use the word "NO," and do not criticize your birds when you are not satisfied with their pronunciation. The budgies do not understand the context.

SHOW your pleasure when your feathered friends mimic the first sounds, and then give them an extra treat.

INTELLIGENCE is enhanced by play, fun, and active learning. "Talk pills" that are supposed to make the birds more intelligent are useless. It is better to invest money in new toys and love your little pets just as they are, even though they may turn out to be less linguistically talented.

Budgerigars as Speech Artists

Budgerigars are one of the best "talkers" among parrots, but not all of them learn to "talk." Generally it can be said that females rarely ever talk. They seem to enjoy it much more when males serenade them. On the other hand, budgerigar males have a very large sound repertoire and learn new sounds quickly. Budgerigars vocalize very fast and at a high frequency. Therefore, it is often easier for children to understand budgerigars.

› In order to support and enhance the possible talent of your budgerigars, you should start out with simple, short words and sentences. A prerequisite for learning is a healthy budgerigar that lives in a stimulating environment.

› Make the communication with the bird easier by always linking certain actions to the same, simple sentences, for instance: *"Would you like a carrot? Please!"*

› Pronounce the word the budgie is supposed to learn very enthusiastically and with a high voice. At that moment your budgies will stop twittering and look at you attentively. They will be listening to you and learning.

› Then gradually link more and more activities with certain words, and strongly praise your budgerigars when they make the first attempts to "speak." Always repeat the same words during certain activities, but do not repeat the very same sentence for an hour—that will be boring for the birds, and they will stop listening.

In spite of all that, there is no guarantee that your birds will talk. Just as it is difficult for us to learn a foreign language, a particular budgerigar may have also reached its limitations.

Body Language: Understanding the Signals

Budgerigars have a well-defined body language that indicates a great deal about these birds.

Everything is fine! A budgerigar that is relaxed and in a good mood sits on its perch in an upright position and on both legs; its plumage lies smoothly against the body or is slightly fluffed up; and the bird vocalizes softly. A pleasantly excited bird raises its head feathers, the pupils narrow, and the chest is pushed out.

Building confidence. If a bird is scared, the plumage tightly hugs the body, making the bird appear longer and thinner. Many budgerigars will not move about when they are scared, hoping that they are not seen. If a bird is seriously frightened, the wings are slightly raised so to be ready for immediate take-off. Should this be the way that your bird is behaving, you will need to work on confidence building measures; presumably, your budgerigar may have had some bad experiences with humans. You will need to withdraw to a distance where the bird is starting to relax again. As a visual aid you can mark with a strip of masking tape the distance where the bird begins to get scared again. Always offer your budgie a treat when you approach it. This way you can gradually—step-by-step—work your way close to the bird until it starts trusting you.

Well-being: The budgerigar is relaxed. It is resting, fluffed-up, and will soon doze off.

After resting, first some stretches—then play and fun is on the agenda.

Grooming Makes Friends

Even when pet budgerigars are kept in flocks, genuine friendships tend to develop between individual birds. This occurs principally among males. Courtship displays and feeding fortify such friendships, which remain unaffected even during a relationship with a female. Social bonds within the group are established by the birds principally through mutual preening, an activity that takes up a large part of the budgerigars' day. To groom, one budgerigar will slowly approach another and push its head toward the other bird. If there is some attraction between the birds, then mutual preening will commence. Such intensive grooming of the plumage also serves to firm up the bond within a pair. Particularly pronounced is head preening among the birds, because that part of the plumage cannot be reached by the budgies by themselves.

That is my millet! Envy over food is not an alien concept to budgerigars. Food treats are defended against competitors with bites and kicks.

When It Comes to Food, All Friendships Are Off

In spite of all friendships, budgerigars can be very resentful of others when there is food involved, and will vehemently defend a treat that was given to them.

Similarly, a favorite branch is not necessarily shared with just any budgerigar that comes flying past. A raised leg and a brief threatening with the beak, as well as slightly raised wings, clearly suggest: *"This is my branch, go fly elsewhere."* Yet, serious conflicts among budgerigars are rare, and if they do occur, it is principally among females when they are ready to breed and the argument is over a nesting site. Therefore, it is advisable to always have more nest boxes available for the birds than there are pairs. Giving the birds a choice will inevitably avoid arguments. If a budgerigar suddenly becomes aggressive for unknown reasons, the bird is probably sick and should

immediately be taken to a veterinarian.

Sometimes even rather self-assured budgerigars will start to chase smaller or insecure siblings from their perches. Should this happen you should provide as many perches as possible and distribute the food over several feeding sites, so that weaker birds can find sufficient food. Sometimes it happens that smaller budgerigars develop into particularly "streetwise" birds.

With so much social contact, budgerigars need regular resting periods. Usually they prefer their favorite perch or branch for sleeping, and there they vocalize softly to themselves. They fluff up their plumage and pull up one leg. Eventually the soft vocalization turns into a gentle twitter, which then changes into beak grinding. That is a sign of total relaxation. The eyes close and the head withdraws under a wing. Your budgie has sung itself to sleep.

Adventure: Free Flight

As mentioned earlier, budgerigars are aerial acrobats and will enjoy some free flight time every day. However, do not attempt to free-flight your birds unless you are willing to take the time and necessary precautions to ensure their safety. Ideally, this free flight should be incorporated in the daily activity cycle. Once your pets become accustomed to the scheduled time, getting them in and out of the cage will become easier.

Take precautions. It is important that the room is absolutely safe and has sufficient landing sites. A child's room is only of limited suitability, because children tend to forget that the birds are flying freely in the open and accidents can happen. Often a budgie escapes through doors that are suddenly opened and subsequently the bird does not find its way back home. Therefore, discuss the free flight time with the entire family in some detail.

Budgerigars are high performance fliers. Risky flight maneuvers, somersaults, and loops are natural components of their aerial antics. A prerequisite, however, is optimal care of the plumage.

Successful Free Flight

The free flight should be particularly exciting so that it provides sufficient diversity to life in a cage. Moreover, budgerigars should move about as much as possible. For that reason you establish landing sites as far away from the cage as possible. Allow sufficient time for your bird to exercise and burn off energy.

Free Flight Sports Course: The various landing sites encountered by the birds during their free flights should also be fitted with numerous pieces of "exercise equipment": a spiral is a seesaw at the same time and affords a great opportunity for running up and down. There also need to be toys, so that the free flight becomes the high point of the day. Triangles are very popular with budgerigars, and if there is also a bell in the middle of the flight path, the budgies will be perfectly happy.

Easy return: Many budgerigar owners have problems getting the birds back into their cage after the free flight. A large cage that has a very large door with an integrated landing perch takes the pressure out of such a situation, because a large opening facilitates the return of the birds into the cage. Top off food and water containers and place a piece of millet inside the cage so that the birds will see it. Now place the birds back inside their cage, praise the birds loudly, and slowly fold up the landing door. If this does not work the first time around, attend to some other things. Then, a few minutes later, make another attempt. Under these circumstances, it pays off not to be in a hurry. Your budgies will quickly learn that it is in their best interest to work along with you. There is no point in putting the birds under any pressure. They move away when you approach and a pointless chase will develop. Confidence will then be destroyed, and after the next free flight the birds will not let you put them back into their cage.

Avoid the Dangers of Free Flight

TIPS FROM THE
BUDGERIGAR EXPERT
Hildegard Niemann

TILTING (PIVOT-HUNG) WINDOWS and open doors can lead to injuries, and birds can escape.
CARPETS with fringing loops that are too large can entrap the claws of budgerigars.
COOKING FUMES, sprays, and aromatic candles cause damage to the respiratory organs of budgerigars and can even be fatal. Overheated Teflon pans give off a deadly odorless gas that is fatal to birds.
GLASSES AND VASES are inviting to drink out of and so can become dangerous traps for a bird that inadvertently falls in and is then unable to free itself. Remove all drowning dangers.
ELECTRICAL CORDS AND OUTLETS are invitations for female budgies to gnaw on. Unplug cords when possible, and monitor your bird at all times.
TOXIC INDOOR PLANTS can be fatal. Replace them with plants that are non-toxic. Safe plant lists are available online.
CANDLES must not be lit during free flight.
NEVER SMOKE cigarettes in the same room as your budgerigars. After smoking, wash your hands before touching your budgies.

Whatever Is Fun!

In the wild, budgerigars spend a large part of the day flying to sites where there is food and looking for water. In our home, our feathered friends have a much easier life. Because they hardly ever have to search for food, they have more time to play and romp around. Budgerigars are temperamental energy bundles with a well-developed inclination for playing. In order to keep play habits within controllable boundaries and to promote the intelligence of the birds, you have to show some imagination. And here you have to keep in mind that every budgerigar has its particular preferences that you will need to take into consideration.

Budgerigar School—The Basics

Budgerigars learn principally through watching. Their eyes will follow you everywhere, and it is not uncommon for them to sit on your shoulder to watch more closely what you are doing. Take advantage of this trait and start teaching a few tricks once or twice every day. Always proceed systematically to ensure teaching success.

› If you are teaching your budgies to ring a small bell, start the training by ringing the bell yourself. Each bird will quickly follow this example. From that point on always praise the bird when it rings the bell and immediately give it a treat. From then on you should structure the path to the bell with increasing complexity so that it becomes a real adventure course. At the end of each successful attempt the birds always get the awaited piece of millet and lots of praise.

› Budgerigars need a lot of exercise to remain physically fit and so not to become fat. If you free-flight your birds, then teach them the commands "Come" and "Fly": Two persons stand opposite each other. One is holding the budgie on his or her finger and hands the bird over to the other person, while saying the command "Fly." The other person replies with "Come," and the bird is given lots of

Ladders and swings are ideal jumping off points when budgerigars are heading on to new adventures; however, sometimes they also serve as a resting place.

praise. Then you slowly increase the distance between yourself and the other person, so that the budgerigar has to fly in order to get over to the other person. This game is fun to play with children.

› The "ladder game" is a fun exercise for flighted and non-flighted birds alike. Once your budgie learns to perch comfortably on your finger, place the index finger of your other hand lightly against its lower chest and say "Step up." When it does, praise it lavishly and repeat the process. This climbing game not only provides great exercise, but it also reinforces the "Step-up" command, a valuable tool for retrieving your pet when you wish to return it to its cage or play stand.

› The search for food is an innate behavioral trait in budgerigars, and it is important to satisfy this instinct. Therefore, turn the search for food into a game. This is wonderful for wing-clipped birds on a play stand. Place sorrel and a few pieces of carrot beneath hollowed-out and upside-down coconut shells, skewer a few pieces of beet onto a slice of kohlrabi, or suspend an apple from a fruit skewer. Hide berries under paper cups. Let your bird seek out and earn its treats.

› Some budgerigars love to take toys apart and then immediately and with great speed throw all the parts about. Clean off a table completely and then spread out an assortment of small toys suitable for budgerigars. These can be little toy cars, lattice balls, ballpoint pens without their cartridge, clothespins, or empty toilet rolls. Soon your little feathered friend will join you and will take great delight in pushing everything off the table. It is your task then to pick everything up off the floor; so that—you guessed it—the bird can push it all off the table once again.

› Very popular among all parrots and parakeets is an old children's game: peek-a-boo! Take a towel (but not one with stripes; stripes mean danger for the birds) and hold it in front of your face. Then

Fruits and vegetables can make fun toys. Most budgerigars are willing to make that extra effort to climb or fly for such a treat.

Understanding and Respect

WITHOUT PRESSURE Never force budgerigars to play. Playing should be fun and must not involve pressure from you. When a budgerigar turns away or takes off, it is afraid of a toy or is tired and inattentive, so leave the bird alone. It has clearly indicated to you that it does not want to play, and *that* you have to respect.

BE CONSIDERATE Teach your children to understand these signals. This does not mean that the budgerigar does not enjoy the company of its owner; it is just not in the mood to play. Keeping budgerigars also involves learning to be patient.

lower it very slowly and call out "peek-a-boo" when the birds see you. Then immediately pull up the towel to cover your face again. You will see your budgerigars laughing!

The Most Fun Toys

As far as budgerigar toys are concerned, one distinguishes between mobility, intelligence, and destruction toys.

Mobility toys include spirals, swings, and triangles. If possible, these should always be attached at the highest point inside the cage, so that maximum room remains available to the bird for swinging and playing.

Intelligence toys are supposed to stimulate the *thinker* among our feathered friends. Apart from commercially available toys, one can also place intellectual demands on the birds with homemade toys. For instance, place a piece of millet in an empty toilet tissue roll and then close it off with some paper towel at both ends. Then your budgie has to tear out the paper towel first before it can

1 WELL OCCUPIED Budgerigars have highly developed color vision, and need colorful toys so that they remain mentally alert. In addition, colorful wooden toys also stimulate the chewing instinct and divert the attention of, principally, females from furniture and wallpaper. In order to make new things attractive for cautious budgerigars, one can decorate them with herbs; that way they are irresistible to the birds.

2 BATHING AND NIBBLING Wet leafy vegetables are ideal toys for birds that may be reluctant to bathe. Especially dark-green vegetables that are rich in vitamin A; budgerigars really like to shred those to pieces. When they are wedged between the cage bars or wrapped around a perch, even those birds that dislike fresh greens become vegetable fanatics.

3 FITNESS TOYS Triangles, swings, and spirals are essential when keeping budgerigars. The little Australian birds are inclined to get fat and so require a lot of exercise in order to stay healthy. Select only toys that have a single suspension point so that the birds can sharpen their sense of balancing. If it should happen that a bell also rings, the happiness of the budgie will be complete.

get to the treat. An empty paper bag can be readily converted into a magnificent *piñata*. Put some grains, a bit of millet, and a few slices of carrot and apple inside the paper bag; the remainder of the bag is then filled with toilet paper. Your budgie can then enjoy tearing the paper apart and will then find a tasty treat to munch on.

Destruction toys are given to budgerigars so that the birds can gnaw on them, tear them apart, or simply chew them to pieces. This keeps the bird's beak properly trimmed, and, especially in females, toys like that can sufficiently satisfy their innate chewing instinct. In addition, you should also offer your budgerigars small, fresh branches on which the birds can chew to their hearts' content. Similarly, commercially available toys with large components of leather, cotton, or sisal can keep your budgies busy for quite a while.

Everything that makes a lot of noise: Budgerigars love little bells and other toys that make noise. In fact, nowadays many budgie toys already include components that ring or rattle. When these are attached to swings or are suspended from the roof of the cage, the birds will be definitely happy.

Caution: You must make sure, though, that those non-destructible toys are not too heavy (e.g., made of acrylic material). Such toys could injure a bird when it—during play—swings back and hits them. Similarly, mirrors have absolutely no place in a cage. The budgerigars think their reflection is another bird and will then continuously try to feed it. This creates an unhealthy preoccupation.

Toys Must Be Safe

Only buy those toys that are designated specifically for budgerigars. This is essential. Your bird will not be able to play optimally with toys designed for larger parrots. Moreover, large toys can hurt your budgerigar by swinging back or falling onto the bird.

Do not buy any secondhand (used) toys. Your budgerigars deserve clean and safe toys.

Double-check the suspension mechanism for damage and rust. Can the beak or claws of the birds become trapped in the device?

Double-check the individual components of all toys for their strength. Can the bird remove certain parts and swallow them?

Avoid toys with long cotton strings that can entangle your bird. You should only offer toys with sisal strings or short cotton bunches that are less likely to entrap a playful bird.

Only purchase leather and metal components for assembling your own toys in the pet shop trade. If any toy contains unsuitable, chemically treated parts, your birds could be poisoned. Every week you need to check all toys and replace those parts that are defective.

Breeding Your Budgerigar

Budgerigars breed whenever the environmental conditions are such that there will be sufficient food for the young. In captivity, this means budgies can breed at any time of the year.

Courtship: This is an exciting time for all those who keep budgerigars. The males make intensive efforts to get the attention of females; they try to impress them with aerial acrobatics and serenade their favorite female with raised feathers and narrowed pupils. This type of singing, referred to as "warbling," leads to an increase in hormone levels in females and induces courtship behavior. In males, warbling promotes increased sperm production. The initially hesitating female eventually responds to the courting male and accepts being fed by him. Shortly thereafter the first mating acts can be seen, when the male climbs onto the back of the female.

Critical partners: Female budgerigars are rather selective. Young, inexperienced males are abruptly rejected, because they are too eager and do not have the patience yet for an intense courtship. On the other hand, it appears that older females are more readily accepted by males. That makes sense, because experienced sex partners are more likely to raise the progeny successfully than inexperienced ones. Young males can already breed after they are approximately 10 weeks of age. This is an adaptation to the sparse environment budgerigars normally live in. Females can also reproduce at a rather young age; however, one should really wait with the first brood until the female is at least one year old. If females are bred too young they can become egg-bound due to a lack of calcium or a still immature endocrine (hormone) system.

Nest cave: As soon as the usually rather stable relationship between budgerigars has been established, the female starts to look for a suitable nesting site. Every small crack and crevice is checked out to see whether there is some sort of cave behind

Little charmer: With a song, raised feather, and a thrown-out chest, the male is courting a female.

Critical tenants: The future brood cave is being thoroughly inspected; after all, both partners must ultimately be satisfied with it.

Tender loving care: Even the youngest are cared for with much dedication. The chicks hatch at intervals of two days and will then grow up quickly.

it that could be used as a nesting site. In captivity, wooden nest boxes are the preferred location.

Incubation and Development of Chicks

Now the time has come to provide the female with a nest box. If you have several females, there should be twice as many nest boxes as there are females. This way you avoid fighting among the birds. Once the females have decided on their respective nest boxes, you should remove all remaining, empty nest boxes. From then on each female will spend much time in her nest box, gnawing on it and also taking in more food. During the period of incubation and while rearing chicks, females require a lot of calcium (*cuttlefish bone*) for developing hard egg shells, for contractions of the oviduct, and for supplying the young. In

addition to the normal diet, you should also offer germinating seeds and rearing food; both have a higher fat content.

The eggs are laid in two-day intervals, until the total clutch of four to six eggs is complete. The first chick usually hatches after 18 days, and its siblings will follow in intervals of two days. At the beginning the chicks, with a weight of .07 to .1 ounce (2 to 3 grams), are still naked and blind, but they will open their eyes during the second week of their life, and in the third week they are already as heavy as their parents. During the first few days the chicks are fed and kept warm exclusively by the mother; later the father will also take part in providing food for the young. At an age of one week, the chicks should be banded, and after about a month the young are fledged.

Care and Health

Budgerigars are cleanliness fanatics. They spend a large part of the day cleaning their plumage, feet, and beak, because the condition of their body is vitally important for their survival in the wild.

Complete Body and Health Care

In their natural environment, budgerigars are totally reliant on meticulously cared for plumage, so that they are able at any time to fly and escape from predators. In the wild, these birds do not come in contact with their droppings or with damaged feathers lost during the molt, because of their way of life; but this is different when we are keeping these birds as pets in our home.

D.I.Y. Body Care

Budgerigars look after their own health, by preening their feathers for a large part of each day. Each feather—whether large or small—is cleaned and neatly returned to its proper place. Sometimes budgerigars will chew on a particular branch until only a pointed section remains. On that the birds will scratch their head and the region around the eyes. But rest assured, budgerigars are indeed precision workers, who know precisely when to use their beak and when to use this particular grooming aid.

Feather-for-Feather

As high performance athletes, budgerigars always make sure that they are constantly in top shape; for that reason, most of the attention is given to the plumage. Although the body is completely covered with feathers, these make up only about 5 to 10 percent of the body weight. The plumage of budgerigars consists of soft (*pinnulate*) down feathers and colorful contour feathers, which include the flight (pinion) feathers and fletching feathers. The down feathers serve as insulation and for the maintenance of an aerodynamic body shape. The flaps of the contour feathers consist of fine lateral rays, with cross braces that reach into each other, similar to those used in zippers. When these connections are not clean they do not properly fit into each other. It then becomes difficult for a budgerigar to maintain its body temperature or even to fly properly. In order to maintain these structures, the bird produces a special grooming oil in its preening gland (*uropygial* gland) at the base of the tail. The bird massages that oil into the plumage in order to keep it healthy and water-resistant.

Among Friends: Mutual Grooming

If for some reason a budgerigar cannot reach certain sections of its plumage, for instance, parts of the head—no problem! With an appropriate

request, a bird turns toward its partner for help as needed. It is deemed to be a large compliment for you, when your budgie starts to preen you: eyebrows, beard hairs, and ears are lovingly nibbled on and the hairs are properly arranged. When this happens, make sure that the little bird does not come into direct contact with mucus or hairspray, which could be harmful to him. If your budgie permits it, you can express your gratitude with an intensive head scratching.

Cleaned from Beak to Tail

Plumage care is not all: body care starts with the beak, which grows continuously throughout the life of the bird and needs to be constantly worn down. In order to keep their beak in optimal condition, budgerigars need to be given plenty of chew toys or non-toxic branches to chew on. Frequently, budgerigars also clean their beak by rubbing it along the perch they are sitting on. Therefore, perches should always be arranged in such a way that the birds cannot soil them from above with their own droppings. Simultaneously, perches also serve in the care of claws. The sharp claws are constantly ground down by the rough tree bark, and the sensitive soles of the feet are massaged at the same time. Another feature budgerigars will enjoy very much is a little landscaped dish with coarse gravel, rocks, and some bird sand, where they can search for food and also wear down their claws.

Spic-and-span: a perfect plumage is the best life insurance. Each feather is cleaned meticulously.

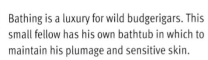
Bathing is a luxury for wild budgerigars. This small fellow has his own bathtub in which to maintain his plumage and sensitive skin.

Beak care is a must: Especially after enjoying a good meal, the birds will clean their beaks on a branch.

The Regular Bath

The natural, wild environment of budgerigars is very dry, and there the opportunities for a bath in peace are indeed rare. That may well be the reason why many pet budgies are distinctly reluctant to take a bath. The birdbath in front of the cage is ignored, and the birds have a lot of respect for the plant mister. Since budgerigars clean themselves thoroughly every day, it is not necessary to let them have a daily bath; however, once a week the birds should be encouraged to take a bath, because it serves to support body hygiene and it is an additional activity. A few tricks can persuade the reluctant bather to overcome its dislike for bathing water. Many budgerigars avoid birdbaths of all kinds. Such birds should once a week be given a handful of dripping wet (organic) lettuce or green cabbage leaves inside their cage. The small parrots will rummage through the wet leaves, rubbing their chest plumage and under their wings with great enthusiasm. The leaves can be put in a shallow earthenware bowl, where the bottom is covered with water. Place this bowl in such a position along the bottom of the cage that it cannot be soiled with bird droppings from above. Gradually you decrease the number of leaves and give more water, so that the birds get a wet belly toiling among the leaves. Use room temperature water; budgerigars have a high body temperature and therefore they tend to dislike warm water.

The Cage: Always Neat and Clean

The cage is the playpen of our budgerigars, where they spend a lot of time. It goes without saying that it must be clean. Yet, that is not always so easy, because budgerigars will "drop something" every 30 minutes or so. Leftover food and small fecal balls will quickly stick to cage bars and various narrow gaps along the cage floor and structure. **Cleaning must be thorough.** It is not enough simply to scrape the dirt off the cage. This would also destroy the coating of the cage, so that in the long term the cage bars will start to rust. You need to wash the cage and bottom tray with warm water and a mild cleaning agent. Afterwards you will have to rinse the cage with clean water so that the cleaning agent is totally washed off. Very hard and resistant dirt should be soaked for a while, which then makes cage cleaning that much easier.

Nowadays, there are also cages that have a protective mesh covering the bottom tray. This mesh prevents the birds from becoming soiled by

Wellness at home: Cleanliness and a diverse offering of toys, as well as food and watering sites, are a must. After all, the cage is a play den, rest area, and dining room all rolled into one.

their own droppings while playing on the bottom of the cage. Make sure that the area underneath and around the cage is easy-to-clean. At least once a day you should vacuum around the cage to remove dust and empty grain husks. If you leave leftover food in cracks and corners for a long time, this will soon attract flour or mill moths and other food scavengers, which are difficult to get rid of once they have become entrenched. Moreover, such dirt places a burden on your respiratory system as well as that of your birds.

Helpful tip: Do not clean the cage while the birds are still in it. Commence cleaning the cage when your pets are on their play stand or having free flight time. While you are doing your cleaning chores, make sure another family member is watching the birds to keep them safe. When your budgies return to play and feed, the cage is dry and clean again.

Bowls and Toys

Suitable cage accessories make cleaning simple: metal bowls that can be placed in the dishwasher are ideal. It is advisable to get two complete sets, so that feeding and cleaning never become a problem in your hectic daily routine. Items made of plastic—whether bowls or toys—should be frequently examined and fecal matter or chewed-on parts must be removed. Clean everything as thoroughly as possible, because gaps and cracks offer parasites and bacteria an ideal breeding ground. Many crop infections develop because bacteria have become established in tiny cracks and are constantly picked up by the birds while drinking, subsequently causing them to become infected.

Cleanliness Is a Must

WHEN?	WHAT?
DAILY	Clean food and water containers (once or twice a day) Replace cage floor cover (paper or bird-safe substrate) Remove droppings and leftover food from perches Vacuum debris around the cage Soak and wipe off fecal balls
WEEKLY	Remove dirty, defective, or chewed-up branches and toys from the cage Check and clean all remaining toys Change toys and attach new ones (Note: favorite toys always remain in the cage) Bottom tray and mesh must be washed in hot water, and left to dry before reassembling the cage; wipe thoroughly around the cage with a damp sponge or cloth
MONTHLY	Check all landing sites, perch branches, ropes, and swings for dirty and chewed-up components and replace any defective items Wash the entire cage with hot water and leave to dry
YEARLY	Replace the birdbath and bird lamp; check the cage for wear-and-tear, rust, etc.

Prevention Is Important

Budgerigars can reach an age of up to 15 years old. Unfortunately, many do not get to be that old, because they die of some disease after a few years. In order to recognize diseases in time, it is important that you observe your birds closely at least once a day for about ten minutes—if possible, without the birds noticing it. This way you will be able to correctly assess the state of health of your budgerigars and disease symptoms will be more conspicuous to you.

Health Check

Healthy budgerigars will chatter all day long, males significantly more so than females. They go through periods of increased activities and then have extended rest periods, normally at about the same time every day.

With some practice you will soon be able to detect whether your pet is feeling well: is the bird sitting normally on both legs? What do the eyes, *cere* (horny skin above the beak), and beak look like? Does the plumage tightly hug the body and is it clean and shiny? Is the budgerigar feeding normally? What do the droppings look like? In females that are courting and laying eggs, the droppings can be enlarged three-fold. This is not unusual and it will return to normal once the egg-laying phase is over.

Weigh your birds once a week. A shallow kitchen scale is suitable for that. You place a tiny piece of millet on the scale and while the bird is eating you can readily read off its weight. For greatest accuracy, use a scale with a "tare" function, which allows you to place the treat onto the scale and then press tare, which zeroes out the scale so you are weighing just the bird, not the bird and millet. If your pet's weight begins to trend up or down, contact your veterinarian for advice. Weight loss can signal disease, while excess weight gain can cause degenerative diseases. Observe whether your budgerigars react to sounds and how they are

Fitness test: This budgerigar is climbing happily on its branch. So that the bird stays that way, you need to examine your pet regularly to assess its condition.

Fussy eater? You must constantly check whether the budgerigars are actually eating their food or whether they are simply playing with it and losing weight.

A Quiet Farewell

BUDGERIGAR SENIORS THAT are suffering pain from age-related diseases sometimes need to be treated constantly with medication prescribed by a veterinarian. The administration of pain-relieving medication, especially for diseases affecting the joints, can enhance the quality of life of the bird, and so facilitate a nearly pain-free old age.

Yet, even for such budgerigars the day will come when the veterinarian will recommend to relieve the bird from its suffering. Therefore, you should not deny your pet this very last, pain-free gesture. Always remember: Your budgie has had a beautiful, carefree life with you and it has given you a lot of joy.

flying. If a budgerigar loses altitude while in flight or is unable to fly again after it has crash-landed, these are definitive alarm signals. Take the little bird immediately to a veterinarian who specializes in exotic animals.

When a Budgerigar Is Getting Old

Old budgerigars have their special charm: they are very familiar with their owner, they are self-assured, and they are no longer as strenuous to handle as when they were juvenile birds. Many budgie seniors suffer from age-related diseases, such as arthritis, vascular problems, and senility. Some also have difficulties with their vision. Generally, older budgerigars should be taken to an avian veterinarian at half-yearly intervals for an assessment of their condition.

Special care: If you are keeping a flock of budgerigars, you must make sure that the senior birds still get sufficient food, because weak birds and those that are ill are often driven away from food and water. If you notice that an old bird is constantly chased away, you should transfer it three times a day to a separate cage where the bird can eat in peace. It goes without saying that such a cage must be equipped with appropriate perches and toys. Old budgerigars with joint problems require particularly wide branches and sitting facilities, because they like to lie down periodically in order to rest their painful joints. Make sure that there are no wounds or pressure sores anywhere on that part of the feet the bird is sitting on. Place several layers of newspaper, with an old towel on top, on the bottom of the cage, so the bird is not injured should it crash down in the cage. You should also offer lots of climbing facilities in such a cage, in the form of ropes. Many older budgerigars prefer to walk and so avoid exhaustive flying.

Diseases: Recognition and Treatment

Budgerigars are able to hide illnesses for a long time, and we, as their keepers, are often the last ones to notice that our pets are not very well. In recent times, it has also been learned that numerous parrot diseases are caused by virus infections. Therefore, all newly acquired birds must always be kept in isolation, before they come in contact with your other budgerigars. Budgerigars also have a tendency toward the development of tumors, and it is not uncommon for budgerigars to die of such a disease before the age of five years. However, in the meantime, avian (bird) medicine has advanced to such a degree that many tumors can be operated on, and our tough little desert birds generally recover fairly quickly from such an operation. Since we often recognize relatively late that our pet birds are not doing well, an affected bird must be taken to a veterinarian immediately. Do not hesitate; it is better to be safe than sorry.

Spot the Symptoms

> A budgerigar is ill when it sits on its perch on both legs, it is fluffed up, and no longer responds to sounds or when called, and when it suddenly can be handled although it was always usually a rather shy bird.
> Lethargy, tiredness, and undigested food are also signs of an illness.
> Some budgerigars stop feeding and drinking when they do not feel well.
> Foul-smelling feces or diarrhea are also significant signs of an infection.
> Cloudy eyes, a discharge from the nostrils, and frequent sneezing are indicative of a disease.
> If a budgerigar is reluctant to use any extremities, it could have sustained an injury and it will require veterinary attention.

When and How to Visit the Veterinarian

From an age of one year, even when a budgerigar is not sick, it is advisable to take the bird to an

This budgerigar has lost weight and sits lethargically in its cage—it is very sick and must be taken to a veterinarian immediately.

experienced avian veterinarian once a year. Birds younger than a year and "seniors" from ten years and more should be taken to a veterinarian every six months. Make an appointment and write down all the questions you may want to ask (see box to the right).

A small plastic transport box is ideal for taking your bird to the vet. This box should always be seen in your living area, so that the birds will recognize it as something that is of no danger to them. When a visit to the veterinarian is imminent, put a towel inside the box and also install a small perch. The towel must not have any large decorative loops where the claws of a budgerigar can become entangled. When it is cold out, place a towel over the box; during the summer, at high temperatures, put a wet towel over the posterior part of the box. Evaporative cooling will keep the little patient comfortable. If the trip is going to take more than 30 minutes, you should also place food and water in the transport box.

Caution: Although most injuries are best treated by keeping the bird very warm, head injuries are the exception. Budgerigars with head injuries should be kept cool and in the dark and be taken immediately to a veterinarian.

First-Aid Kit for Budgerigars

You should assemble a first-aid kit for your budgerigars so that in the case of illnesses or accidents you can provide immediate help.

› Absolutely essential for the care of a sick budgerigar is an infra-red heat lamp or heating pad. The bird must expend a lot of energy in order to maintain its body temperature in the event of an illness. To make this easier for the bird, you need to install the infra-red heat lamp about 20 inches

---

Checklist for a Veterinarian Visit

TIP FROM THE
BUDGERIGAR EXPERT
Hildegard Niemann

TIME Give yourself sufficient time to visit the veterinarian. You need to calculate the time needed to travel to the veterinarian and back again, and waiting time as well as the time for the actual examination.

IMPORTANT NOTE Take along the bottom tray paper with droppings from the last 24 hours. The droppings can provide important clues as to the health of your budgerigar.

RESOLVE QUESTIONS Make a note of all of your questions and discuss them with your veterinarian. When a point is not clear to you, keep asking until you understand. Avoid questioning the veterinarian during the actual examination, so that he or she can concentrate on the patient.

CORRECT DIAGNOSIS If the veterinarian cannot ascertain the reason as to why a bird is sick, he or she might recommend additional testing, or might treat your bird with a broad spectrum antibiotic until test results are available.

MEDICATION Administer all medication only as per instructions; request that you be shown how to do this while you are still with the veterinarian. If you encounter any problems, you should inform the veterinarian immediately.

(50 cm) away from the cage. Place a towel over half of the cage, so that the patient can select whether he requires additional heat or not.

› A ferric chloride solution can be very helpful for the treatment of injuries. It facilitates blood clotting, and in an emergency it can be used on the budgerigar as first aid, until you reach the veterinarian. Soak a sterile gauze pad with this solution and press it gently onto the wound. **Caution:** the solution stings and the budgie will strenuously resist it!

› Claw and beak scissors, elastic bandages,

adhesive tape, and cotton swabs must be included in this first-aid kit. Thin forceps help with the removal of small foreign bodies.

› For gastrointestinal tract ailments, always seek veterinary advice. Gastrointestinal symptoms are often the first sign of more serious disease processes, and should always be evaluated by an avian veterinarian. Do not use over-the-counter medications, which will only suppress the symptoms, not cure the disease.

› Vitamin and calcium preparations are used as support during the molt and for infections. These preparations should be kept cool and dry as recommended by the manufacturer.

› Store this first-aid kit so that it is quickly and easily accessible in case of an emergency. The telephone number of your veterinarian and a 24-hour emergency vet service should be available right next to the telephone. Budgerigars are very small birds with a high metabolic rate. When they become sick, the owner has little time to respond effectively.

Tender Loving Care

Sick budgerigars need a lot of rest and warmth (see page 55). With that in mind it is best to move the little bird to a quiet environment (separate room) until it has recovered. While the budgie is ill you should offer energy-rich food and it should get millet every day. Many sick budgerigars feed exclusively on millet and then recover rather quickly. Never add medication to the drinking water unless as directed by your veterinarian; instead,

Mange, a parasitic infestation caused by mites, is easy to treat. With early therapy there are no residual damages.

administer it drop-by-drop via a clean disposable syringe (2 to 5 ml) without a needle, directly into the beak. This is the only way you can be assured that the bird receives the prescribed amount of medication necessary for the bird to get well again. Always administer the medication silently and afterwards give the bird a rest, and follow any instructions given by the veterinarian exactly.

The Molt

Bird feathers do not last indefinitely, and especially birds from arid and desert regions must be able to cope with the fact that their plumage bleaches out, or becomes brittle and frayed. Once feathers have been worn out they must be replaced. This process is known as molting (the molt). The molting cycle in budgerigars lasts about nine months. During this period, budgerigars replace their entire plumage. Old feathers fall out or are pulled out by the bird when they start to itch. When this involves the large flight feathers as well as the tail feathers, the budgerigars go through a strenuous period. The birds become tired and also somewhat surly. Their body must produce, from scratch, all of the material needed to grow the new feathers. Therefore, a healthy diet and appropriate supplements are especially necessary during the molt.

Hand-tame budgerigars enjoy it very much when new feathers around the head region, which are still encased by whitish sheaths, are manually opened up. To do that you gently pick up a feather between thumb and index finger and then gently rub the fingers together. The feather sheath will disintegrate into a fine, white powder.

At a Glance: The Most Common Diseases of Budgerigars

DISEASE	SYMPTOMS	PATHOGENS / CAUSES
French Molt (AKA Budgerigar Fledgling Disease)	Juvenile birds lose their flight and tail feathers; permanent flight disability. Can be highly contagious to other psittacine birds.	Avian polyomavirus; Psittacine Beak and Feather Disease (PBFD)
Going Light Syndrome	Emaciation, diarrhea, undigested grain in droppings, increased appetite	Fungus (*Macrorhabdus ornithogaster*); Proventricular Dilatation Disease (PDD); enterobacter infection.
Crop inflammations *(Sour Crops)*	Frequent vomiting, sticky head feathers, slow passage of food from crop	Numerous fungal or bacterial infections; foreign object impaction.
Parrot Fever *(Psittacosis or chlamydiosis)*	Respiratory distress, severe diarrhea, green urates, paralysis, sudden death	*Chlamydophila psittaci*, transmittable to humans, must be reported to Health Authorities.
PBFD "Psittacine Beak and Feather Disease" *(Psittacine Circovirus Disease)*	Plumage changes (clubbed, deformed, or missing feathers, increasing in severity from molt to molt), crumbling or rotting beak, diarrhea, apathy, emaciation	Circovirus; occurs in acute or chronic forms. Birds with chronic form can survive with care, but must be isolated for life from other birds.

Budgerigars in Distress

Even with the best of care and attention there can be problems in the life of your budgie. While many of these problems can readily be resolved with minor adjustments to the maintenance regimen, sometimes questions arise that puzzle even an expert.

When a bird's partner dies. The death of a budgerigar's partner is a heavy loss to the bird left behind. Usually the remaining bird calls for hours for the departed bird and looks for it throughout the home. After some days the bird gives up the search, apparently realizing that the partner will not return. Find a new companion for your lonely budgerigar so that your pet does not feel so alone. Here you need to remember the quarantine requirements (see page 24).

Shoving off . . . budgerigars react seven times faster than humans, and they can quickly escape through an open door or window.

A bird has escaped. Budgerigars are incredibly agile and fast flyers. It is not uncommon that a bird escapes through a tilted window or through an open door. Presumably such a bird is not likely to find its way back home again. Once you have gotten over the initial shock, you should go out with a small portable cage, looking for your pet within an area of about one mile, loudly calling for it. Put up posters with a picture of your budgerigar, and inform common meeting points in the vicinity (bakeries, drug stores, etc.) that you are missing a budgerigar. Usually escaped budgerigars are found exhausted after a day or two and are then handed into an animal shelter. You should also leave your address details with such a shelter in case your bird turns up.

Separate quarreling birds. Generally speaking, budgerigars are peaceful birds, and it is indeed rare if one bird simply does not like another bird. Nevertheless, arguments can arise, for instance, when there are more females than males in the same cage. Continuous arguing and chasing away (or being chased away) from feeding sites can be a burden on the whole flock. In such a case it is advisable to purchase another cage with a (removable) dividing panel down the middle to keep the quarreling birds apart. Such dividing panels can be inserted and pulled out again within seconds. This way, the birds can use the entire cage while you are at home, and then be separated when you are unable to supervise them.

Diagnosis: Unable to fly. Causes for being unable to fly can be—apart from the French Molt—broken bones, as well as an advanced age of the budgerigar. Provide more climbing opportunities for such a budgerigar by arranging ropes, ladders, and branches in such a way that the "pedestrian" bird can walk through the cage area. More problematic for budgerigars are falls whereby the bird lands on its sternum (breast bone), causing bone fractures. Place a double layer of old towels below a landing site. These can be changed daily and will cushion any impact.

Weight loss required. Many budgerigars are overweight and consequently suffer from fat bulges. Such fat accumulations are dangerous and can lead to serious disease problems. Sometimes such budgies have to be put on a strict diet. When the birds are kept in pairs or in a flock, this is not particularly easy to do, because the affected bird will need to eat a different food than its siblings. Here, too, another cage with a dividing wall is the answer. The birds can then be fed individually after the separating cage panel is put in place. Afterwards the panel is pulled out, and the birds can play together again.

No breeding desired. Females wanting to breed can be real pests. Each tiny hole, nook, or crevice is checked out, no matter how small, to see whether it could be useful as a nesting site. The budgie owner has no other choice but to close off every hole or crevice during the free flight period. Moreover, offer such females lots of soft wood to chew on and make sure that the birds have at least 12 hours of rest at night in a dark room. That lowers the hormone levels of females.

Depression. Budgerigars are happy birds by nature, yet they can also encounter emotional disturbances. An otherwise active bird suddenly sits lethargically in its cage and does not like to play or even chatter. If the veterinarian confirms

Older budgerigars that are sick are often chased away from food. Feed them separately and monitor their weight.

that there is nothing physically wrong with the bird, you can assume that the budgie is depressed. Now you will have to spend a lot of time with this bird, monitor its relationship to the companion bird(s), and offer a lot of interesting toys. Music, laughter, and lots of sporting activities will help the bird regain its joy in life.

Expert consultant required. When keeping budgerigars, various problems can occur that may be too difficult for the budgie owner to handle, and these may require professional help. Many budgerigars are afraid of human hands and the birds will panic when approached. Similarly, budgerigars that suffer from cage bonding (see page 24), stereotypic behavior, and feather pulling problems should be reviewed by a behavioral therapist.

INDEX

RESOURCES

Budgerigars on the Internet

> Budgerigar Association of America (The BAA)
www.tailfeathersnetwork.com
Listings of all the affiliated budgie clubs.
> Budgerigar Association of America
www.budgerigarassociation.com
Publishers of the magazine *Budgerigar Journal*. Membership application, band order form, articles, and photographs.

Useful Addresses

American Budgerigar Society
141 Hill Street Extension
Naugatuck, CT 06770

Important Information

> Sick budgerigar. If your bird shows symptoms of a disease, it belongs in the hands of a veterinarian.

> Cross contamination. Only a few bird diseases are transmittable to humans. Advise your family physician of your animal contact. This is particularly important for influenza-like illnesses.

> Allergy and asthma. Some react to feather and feather dust. If you are uncertain, consult your family physician prior to the purchase of a budgerigar.

American Federation of Aviculture
P.O. Box 56218
Phoenix, AZ 85079

Aviculture Society of America
P.O. Box 5516
Riverside, CA 92517

Bird Clubs of America
P.O. Box 2005
Yorktown, VA 23692

Books

Birmelin, Immanuel, and Annette Wolter. *The Parakeet Handbook.* Hauppauge, New York: Barron's Educational Series, Inc., 2000.

Birmelin, Immanuel. *My Parakeet and Me.* Hauppauge, New York: Barron's Educational Series, Inc., 2001.

Viner, Bradley. *All About Your Budgerigar.* Hauppauge, New York: Barron's Educational Series, Inc., 1999.

Wolter, Annette and Monika Wegler. *The Complete Book of Parakeet Care.* Hauppauge, New York: Barron's Educational Series, Inc., 1994.

Magazines

Bird Talk
P.O. Box 57437
Boulder, CO 80323

Birds USA
P.O. Box 55811
Boulder, CO 80322

Acknowledgment

The publisher and author would like to express their thanks and appreciation to Wagner's Papageien-Paradies, Geilenkirchen, for their support of the photographic productions (cage and toys) as well as to Mr. Karl-Heinz Lambert for his outdoor photographs and to Dr. Carlo Manderscheid for the illustrations of disease symptoms.

Photographs provided by:

All photographs in this book have been provided by Oliver Giel, except for
Karl-Heinz Lambert: Pages 6, 8
Sabrina Kaiser: Pages 14, 45 (right)
Dr. Carlo Manderscheid: Pages 54, 56

Editor-in-Chief: Anita Zellner
Editor: Jutta Weikmann
Associate Editor: Barbara Kiesewetter
Photo-Editor: Natasha Klebl
Production: Petra Roth
Translated by: U. Erich Friese

All inquiries should be addressed to:
Barron's Educational Series, Inc.
250 Wireless Boulevard
Hauppauge, New York 11788
www.barronseduc.com

Library of Congress Control Number: 2008920979

ISBN-13: 978-0-7641-3897-3
ISBN-10: 0-7641-3897-9

Printed in China

9 8 7 6 5 4 3 2 1

About the author:

Hildegard Niemann has a degree as a biologist and she freelances as a "Parrot Behavior Consultant." She advises those who keep budgerigars and other parrots on behavior, husbandry, and nutrition. She works as an author and has published numerous specialist articles.

About the photographer

Oliver Giel has specialized in nature and animal photography. He and his partner Eva Scherer work on the production of illustrations for books, periodicals, calendars, and advertising.

What to do in an emergency?

Crash landing

PROBLEM Your budgerigar has fallen behind a shelf or a cupboard and cannot get out on its own. **SOLUTION:** Dim the lights and slowly pull the piece of furniture away. A stick may help the bird climb out on its own. If the bird appears injured in any way, take it to a veterinarian immediately.

Chewing habit

PROBLEM Well-developed chewing instincts together with curiosity often lead to poisonings in budgerigars. **SOLUTION:** If you are worried that your budgie has ingested some poison, take the bird immediately to a veterinarian. Take the material your budgerigar was seen chewing on with you. It may help the veterinarian to come to the correct diagnosis.

Emergency help

PROBLEM You are unable to look after your budgerigar because of, for instance, illness. **SOLUTION:** Make arrangements with relatives or friends for help. Leave written instructions, detailing feedings, daily activities, address of your veterinarian, the birds' preferences and what frightens them.

Escaped

PROBLEM The bird enjoys tormenting you by not returning to its cage. **SOLUTION:** If you are certain that the cage is optimally fitted out, and that the bird is not afraid of it, you can resort to a few tricks to lure the bird back into its own home. Lower the light and offer your bird an opened transport box. This serves as a substitute "shuttle" back to the cage. A piece of foxtail millet helps to give special appeal to such a utensil. It also helps if this box is an accustomed sight to the bird. Once the bird has walked into the transport box, you can return it to its cage.

Entangled

PROBLEM During free flight your pet has become entangled with its claw in a curtain. **SOLUTION:** Place a kitchen towel over your hand and hold the struggling bird with it. Then slowly remove the claw from the curtain. Do not talk to the budgerigar while doing this, because the bird would associate your voice with this unpleasant event.